IMAGES OF
OXFORD

IMAGES OF
OXFORD

Compiled by
Peter Farr and Don Chapman

Breedon Books
Publishing Company
Derby

First published in Great Britain by
The Breedon Books Publishing Company Limited
44 Friar Gate, Derby, DE1 1DA.
1994

ISBN 1 873626 90 8

Printed and bound by Butler & Tanner, Frome and London.
Covers printed by BDC Printing Services Limited of Derby

Contents

Foreword

OXFORD has boasted a succession of brilliant photographers from the legendary Henry Taunt to the world-renowned 'Tommy' Thomas, now in his 80s and still recording the city's architectural splendours. Consequently, there has been no shortage of picture books to delight the resident and the tourist.

This one, though, is different. For the first time it draws extensively on the thousands of pictures in the *Oxford Mail* photographic library, as well as using photographs from The Centre for Oxfordshire Studies and the Minns Collection. The result, we like to think, is a portrait that it is truer to the spirit of the city where we were born and have lived, give or take a year or two, all our lives.

While it recognises the pomp and circumstance of academic Oxford and the bull-nosed brass of Cowley, it reveals some unexpected facets. By the nature of their employment press photographers – and their editors – are always looking for the picture that tells a story.

The story these pictures tell is, in essence, the story of a small market town which had greatness thrust upon it. People who complain that Oxford does not have a purpose-built concert hall or a Hilton hotel (although it does have the Randolph) overlook the fact that it has a population of only 131,500 people. It is not a Birmingham, a Leeds or a Manchester.

That is part of its charm. Despite its expansion to meet first the demands of the burgeoning university, then those of Lord Nuffield's sprawling motor works, you can still catch glimpses of the green hills beyond as you wander around central Oxford.

Scholar Gipsy country still beckons the resident threading his or her way through the tourist and traffic choked streets on a hot summer's afternoon in much the same way as the first vision of the dreaming spires brings the heart to the mouth of the visitor descending on Oxford.

Small is beautiful. It can also be unbelievably squalid. While students and dons lived in growing luxury as the centuries progressed, a lot of the townspeople under their thumbs went hungry, short of clothes and lived cheek by jowl in tumbledown tenements.

The invention of photography came just in time to record the slums of Oxford before the twentieth century swept them away and you will find plenty of examples of them in these pages. It also came just in time to chronicle the transformation from a sleepy market town, where grass grew between the cobble-stones in the university vacations, into a bustling, industrious city.

The story of Oxford is as inextricably bound up with Lord Nuffield, the cycle shop apprentice who became a multi-millionaire car magnate, as its geography is with the River Thames and its backwaters and tributaries – the playground of academic Oxford and cause, so natives from bracier climes tell us, of the Oxford cough.

The architecture of the university city gives it a timeless quality, a surreal atmosphere where past and present confront one another, like Alice, through the looking glass. In reality change goes on all the time. And ultimately change is what this book is about.

The change that impels the modern to sweep away the old-fashioned. The change that prompts one generation to cover up the handiwork of a predecessor and a later generation to uncover it again. The change in lifestyles, clothing, habits, working practices, leisure activities, houses, streets, whole neighbourhoods.

Even as this book rolls off the presses the bulldozers are sweeping away the old Morris Motors factories that have dominated Oxford for most of the twentieth century and paving the way for a hi-tech development with business parks, superstores, restaurants and the rest.

You can look at the pictures which follow, make the comparisons and decide for yourselves which are odious. One thing is certain. In a few years time somebody else will be able to trawl through the photographic archives at Newspaper House and come up with a selection of pictures which is every bit as fascinating and illuminating as we trust ours is.

Carfax looking south down St Aldate's in 1897. The newly-completed Oxford Town Hall was opened by the Prince of Wales on 2 May 1897. In five years time he was to become King Edward VII.

St Aldate's looking north towards Christ Church on 28 July 1904.

Pembroke Street, St Aldate's, some time before World War Two. Note the straw strewn on the road to muffle the sound of horses' hooves.

Speedwell Street, St Aldate's, before World War One.

Wigmore's dairymen with their carts posing at the corner of St Aldate's and Speedwell Street in the late 1900s. The milk was ladled from the churn into customer's own utensils.

No 28 Cornmarket Street at the corner of Ship Street as it looked at the turn of the century when it was the headquarters of the tea and coffee importers, Harvey Bros & Co.

In the early 1950s, 28 Cornmarket Street was restored to its original seventeenth-century glory. In 1986-87 the adjoining buildings were extensively restored by Jesus College.

Cornmarket Street looking south in the early years of this century.

Cornmarket Street puts the flags out for King Edward VII's Coronation in 1902 – he had been an undergraduate at Christ Church. Notice the horse bus on the left of the picture.

Ship Street looking west to the Plough Inn in Cornmarket Street before Jesus College's new buildings on the south side were built in 1906-08. The Plough closed in 1924 and is now Austin Reed's.

Cornmarket Street before World War One. The Clarendon Hotel, which is already flying the Stars and Stripes, was to become an American Servicemen's Club in World War Two. F.W.Woolworth bought the building in 1939, intending to build a new store on the site, but demolition of the hotel was delayed by the start of the war.

Grimbly Hughes and Co's famous high-class grocery store which dominated Cornmarket Street from 1840 to 1961. It finally fell victim to the supermarkets, but old Oxford students still wax lyrical about its cheese and bacon counters and its Christmas hampers went all over the world.

Cornmarket Street before pedestrianisation in May 1961.

Looking down St Ebbe's towards Cape's, the cash drapers, early this century. In the foreground is G.R.Cooper's hardware and ironmongery store with its distinctive sign 'The Original City Dustpan'.

Cape's Cash Drapery in St Ebbe's shortly before it closed in 1971 to make way for the Westgate development. The firm, founded in the 1870s, was legendary for stocking items other Oxford shops didn't and at one time had a live-in staff.

Queen Street from New Inn Hall Street in the 1930s. Beyond is St Ebbe's Street.

One of the many slum tenements up the side streets of central Oxford: Chaundy's Hall, St Ebbe's, in June 1914.

Blackfriars Road in the 1940s. It was demolished in the 1950s as part of the St Ebbe's redevelopment.

Blackfriars Road, St Ebbe's
in December 1956.

The junction of St Ebbe's and Brewer Street in November 1961, looking down Littlegate Street to what is now the New Centre for the Deaf and Hard of Hearing, which incorporates a medieval gateway.

Shops at the junction of Queen Street and St Ebbe's in April 1959.

January 1960 immediately before the demolition of ten shops at the corner of Queen Street and St Ebbe's to make way for City Council offices with shops beneath.

Church Street, St Ebbe's, now part of the Westgate Centre. On the right is the Oxford Technical School, which grew into Oxford Brookes University.

September 1960 – work is well under
way on the new City Council offices at
the corner of Queen Street and St Ebbe's
Street.

Preacher's Lane, part of
the St Ebbe's
development, in April
1964.

Oxford Archaeological Excavation Committee at work on two medieval tenements – Domus Mirifeld and White Hall – during the St Ebbe's redevelopment in August 1969.

Bus queue in a snowy Queen Street in January 1977.

Castle Street looking east in the early 1900s. The building the chap is cycling past was, in 1910, to become Oxford's first cinema.

Queen Street looking west to Castle Street in August 1907.

Crowds outside the Assize Court at County Hall in New Road during the trial of suffragette Helen Craggs in October 1912. Straw on the road muffled the sound of horses' hooves.

Castle Street changing direction in 1969 as part of the Central Area Redevelopment. The brick building with the turrets was the headquarters of the Salvation Army in Oxford from 1888 to 1970, when it was demolished to make way for new County Council offices.

Mac Fisheries Corner – the junction of Queen Street, Castle Street and New Road in June 1961 from what is now Bonn Square. Later in the decade it was demolished to make way for the Westgate Centre.

The Westgate development in July 1970 looking past the realigned Castle Street to County Hall and Nuffield College. On the left of the picture the Salvation Army Citadel is still standing – just!

Magdalen Street looking south early this century. Next door to the Domestic Bazaar is Emberlin's, a well-known Oxford stationers, with the City and County Registry for Male and Female Servants above, and next door to that is the Taphouse Music Rooms.

Broad Street from its junction with Magdalen Street East at the end of the 1920s. In 1928 conservationists protested bitterly at the demolition of the fine old eighteenth-century house, where the poet W.B.Yeats had lived, to make way for Boswell House. But the developers won.

Broad Street at the end of the last century when it was still possible to see at a glance how it got its name.

Broad Street looking east past the Sheldonian Theatre and Clarendon Building before the building of the Indian Institute at the bottom in the late nineteenth century.

The bottom of Broad Street in the 1930s. The buildings, including the sixteenth-century pub on the corner with Parks Road, were demolished in 1936 to make way for the New Bodleian Library.

Blackwell's world-famous bookshop before the demolition of the Broad Street-Parks Road corner to make way for the New Bodleian Library in the 1930s.

The Mitre Hotel in High Street in about 1880, when it was still one of Oxford's leading coaching inns. It dates from 1300. Notice the Great Western Railway office to the left with the railway dray outside.

Re-laying the road outside the Examination Schools in High Street before World War One. There were few mechanical aids but labour was cheap.

High Street at its junction with Long Wall Street just before World War One, when traffic was light, at least on this particular day.

A much more hectic scene. Traffic and pedestrians thronging High Street in 1961. In August that year workmen installed traffic islands in High Street. They made life less hazardous for dons and students crossing to the Examination Schools.

Hythe Bridge Street looking east towards George Street. The bridge has been falling down for centuries. It last collapsed in 1968, causing the closure of the road for two weeks.

George Street looking west in May 1935 at the time of King George V's Silver Jubilee. On the right is the Apollo, then the New, Theatre.

Threeways House in George Street, a development built by the Oxford and District Co-operative Society Ltd in 1936. The Oxford Milk Bar, run by Oxford and Cambridge Milk Bars Ltd, was there until 1956, when the Co-op opened a radio and television store.

Park End Street at its junction with Rewley Road and Hollybush Row. On the right beyond Butler's is the Eagle Steam Brewery, which Hall's took over in 1897, and further up the street is the warehouse of the removal firm, Archer, Cowley and Co, completed in 1909. The building on the left is the Railway Hotel, which made way for the Royal Oxford Hotel in 1934.

The old LMS Station at the corner of Park End Street and Rewley Road, built for the London and North Western Railway (LNWR) in 1851 by the same team that built the Crystal Palace and incorporating some of the same cast-iron units in the canopy. It closed to passengers in 1951.

Woodstock Road looking north from near the corner of Staverton Road. The picture, taken on 1 June 1903, shows the remains of the grass verge which once ran the entire length of the road.

The Waggon and Horses in Woodstock Road decorated for the Coronation of King George V in June 1911.

The stocks tree at the corner of Cowley Road and Temple Road about the turn of the century. The tree was cut down in 1907.

Cowley Road looking west in April 1941.

South Parade, Summertown, in the 1920s.

South Parade, Summertown, in December 1956, traditionally the suburban shopping centre of North Oxford dons and their wives.

Bridge Street, Osney, under water on 21 June 1903. Being hemmed in by the Thames and its backwaters, Osney Town or Island was prone to flooding.

For delivery vans it was business as usual in 1890 in flooded Lake Street. Flooding was a constant problem in low-lying Oxford before modern drainage.

Cardigan Street, Jericho, on 8 June 1955 after a heavy thunderstorm.

Looking down New College Lane from Catte Street towards the end of the last century before the building of the extension to Hertford College and the 'Bridge of Sighs' linking it to the main college.

THE UNIVERSITY

The Edwardian undergraduate's idea of a good day out. A coach outing about to set off from University College for Wallingford in 1907.

Members of the Bullingdon, reputedly Oxford's most exclusive student club, linking arms with members of the Oxford City Police force outside the Town Hall sometime before World War One.

The University Public Orator presents the Mayor of Oxford, Alderman William Gowers, for his honorary degree at a February 1955 ceremony in the Sheldonian Theatre.

Women students in 'subfusc' – the traditional dress for academic examinations – arriving at the Sheldonian Theatre in October 1955 to receive their degrees.

The Prime Minister Harold Macmillan doffs his hat to applauding spectators as he processes along Beaumont Street for Encaenia, the university's biggest degree ceremony of the year, in 1958. Behind the Conservative premier is Hugh Gaitskell, leader of the Labour opposition. Both became honorary Doctors of Civil Law. It was the first time a premier and leader of the opposition had been honoured at the same time.

The lady on the left seems to know that face. The Chancellor of Oxford University, Harold Macmillan, at the 1965 Encaenia garden party in Trinity College Gardens.

Foreign secretary Selwyn Lloyd sharing a joke with the former Conservative prime minister the Earl of Home in the 1960 Encaenia procession.

Dame Janet Vaughan signs for her honorary degree at the 1967 Encaenia ceremony. About to sign is professor Wolfgang Kunkel.

The 1968 Encaenia Garden Party in St John's College gardens. For the first time for many years it rained continuously.

Heavy rain soon sent guests in search of shelter
underneath the trees and marquee, at the Encaenia
Garden party held in St John's College Gardens in
June 1968.

The Encaenia Garden Party in
Merton College grounds in June
1967. Guests traditionally
received strawberries and cream
with their tea.

Torpids, the spring term college bumping races, taking place on the flooded Thames in February 1904. Supporters had to run along the waterlogged towpath in support of their crews.

A college boatman prepares his crew for the start of an Eights Week Race earlier this century. Notice the newsreel team filming the event with two cameras.

Oriel College barge listing under the weight of the spectators during Eights Week in the early 1900s.

A wartime Oxford University Boat Race crew on the river at Folly Bridge in January 1943. Because of World War Two the annual race took place at Radley, not London.

The crew getting fit for the race.

The scene just after St John's College crew had 'bumped' – the way you move up a place – in the 1961 Summer Eights races. The piles in the water were for the new Donnington Road Bridge.

St Edmund Hall first crew stay head of the river in the 1961 University Summer Eights races. Notice the purpose-built boathouses which replaced the traditional college barges lining the Thames after World War Two.

Students dashing along the towpath in support of their college crews at the 1963 Summer Eights.

Members of the Oxford College Barge Appeal committee in Edwardian Eights Week attire in 1966, attempting to raise money to restore the barges. By this time some of those craft surviving had concrete bottoms and were in terminal decay.

BY THE RIVERSIDE

Jacob Beesley's osier yard by the river upstream of Hythe Bridge about 1874. Mr Beesley stands on the left by a collection of completed eel traps and crayfish creels. His workforce peel osiers or willow wands.

The water mill at Iffley Lock about 1885. It burnt down in 1908.

The Thames at Oxford frozen over in 1895.

Before the Thames Conservancy improved river flows, the Thames froze quite often during the winter. Here is a coach and four on the ice at Folly Bridge in 1891. A coach and six took to the ice in 1895. And an Austin Seven car in 1963.

Salter Bros launch a lifeboat from their yard at Folly Bridge on 23 June 1900. Although Oxford is about as far from the sea as you can get, its residents have always been staunch supporters of the Royal National Lifeboat Institution.

A traffic jam on the Cherwell in the 1920s. Notice the puntsmen punting from 'the Oxford end' of the punt.

Relief keeper I.A.C.West breaking the ice at Iffley Lock in February 1956 to prevent children risking their lives.

College oarsmen do not always pay the Thames the respect it deserves. Schoolboys survey the result of a rowing accident at Iffley in February 1957.

TELLING THE STORY – THE *OXFORD MAIL*

One of the early Austin Seven vans that formed the *Oxford Mail and Times* delivery fleet. In 1934 the expanding newspaper company invested in a fleet of new Morris Cowley vans.

The *Oxford Mail* hit the streets for the first time on 12 December 1928. It was the brainchild of two former Liberal MPs, Oxford businessman and entrepreneur Frank Gray, and Westminster Press boss Sir Charles Starmer. After a brief battle with the well-established weekly, *The Oxford Times*, which tried to bring out a rival daily evening paper, the two companies merged under the Westminster Press banner into what is now Oxford and County Newspapers. The converted furniture warehouse in New Inn Hall Street pictured here became Newspaper House.

The *Oxford Mail* rolling off the basement press at New Inn Hall Street on 12 December 1949 – the paper's 21st anniversary.

In the *Oxford Mail* Reporters' Room at the beginning of the 1950s. On the right is chief reporter Bill Sawyer, renowned for his immaculate shorthand. Standing at the back is Ron Grimshaw, the paper's cricket and rugby correspondent.

Newspaper House in 1954. The central display in the right-hand window shows how Robert Bannister ran the first mile under four minutes at Iffley Road running track on 6 May that year.

A van driver loads *Oxford Mail* in the yard in October 1961.

Shoe Lane off New Inn Hall Street – the only access
to the tiny yard behind Newspaper House from
which the van drivers collected the *Oxford Mail* – in
December 1961.

Oxford Mail tele-ad
girls at New Inn Hall
Street in July 1968.

The expansion of the *Oxford Mail*, the traffic congestion at the city centre and an ageing printing press made life increasingly difficult at Newspaper House. Eventually Oxford and County Newspapers opted to move to purpose-built offices at Osney Mead. Immediately after the *Sports Mail* rolled off the presses on Saturday, 19 February 1972, Pickford's moved in. In the next 24 hours they shifted 50 tons of material in 675 packing cases. On Monday the *Oxford Mail* rolled off the new press at the new Newspaper House. Here sports editor, Arthur Roche, is in duffel-coat checking, as he did every Saturday, the *Sports Mail* as it came off the press. This Saturday, 19 February 1972, it was different. The *Sports Mail* was the last publication to be produced at New Inn Hall Street before the weekend dash to Osney Mead.

The reception desk at Newspaper House shortly before they moved to Osney Mead in 1972.

March 1974 – the old Newspaper House makes way for a new development of shops and offices. The basement press hall is clearly visible. There is a temporary city centre office across the road.

The *Mail* has carried many sensational pictures, none more so than this. Oxford came the nearest it had been to destruction since the seventeenth-century English Civil War at the end of the 1960s. On the night of 23-24 June 1969, Eric Molloy, a 39-year-old self-employed demolition expert, toured central Oxford in a van packed with 36lb of gelignite threatening to blow himself up after being crossed in love. Eventually he returned home to his council house at Alice Smith Square, Littlemore, where he destroyed himself and the house, injuring his wife and two of his children. The picture from the top of Peers School shows his house after the explosion. The van is on the left.

LORD NUFFIELD AND THE CAR WORKS

William Morris's showroom at the bottom of High Street, Oxford, in 1902, the year he showed his first motor cycle in London. Little did the coach and four party realise what the future held in store.

The Oxford car magnate, William Morris, later Lord Nuffield's first office in Longwall Street, which he occupied from 1904 until the move to Cowley in 1913. It remained untouched as he left it until his death in 1963. The bottle of patent medicine reflects a lifelong concern about his health.

Longwall Street garage in 1907. William Morris is in the car on the extreme right.

Another shot of the Longwall Street garage. Again, William Morris is in the car on the right.

Lord Nuffield with the biggest cycle he ever made – for an outsize Oxford cleric. He was only 16 in 1893 when he set up in business on his own.

A different mode of transport. Lord Nuffield being taken for a ride in a sheep-drawn cart at Wingfield Hospital fête in 1930.

The modest office at Cowley, which served as Lord Nuffield's office from 1913 to 1962 – as he left it. The picture he liked so much he bought the original. The barometer was a gift from his eight oldest employees when the millionth Morris car rolled off the line in 1939.

In 1931 Oxford University recognised Lord Nuffield's munificence by making him an honorary Doctor of Civil Law. Here he is arriving for the ceremony with the Vice-Chancellor of the day, Dr F.Homes-Duddon.

At the wheel of a stripped down MG sports car in the 1930s. 'MG' was short for Morris Garages.

Lord Nuffield with Garfield Weston in 1938 at the wheel of the 22nd Morris car, built in 1913 and still going strong.

Lord Nuffield congratulates works manager Mr A.E.Keen on the millionth Morris car to roll off the Cowley production line on 22 May 1939.

Lord Nuffield has a word with test pilot R.Eynell, who has just given the okay to a reconditioned Hurricane fighter plane to return to action in the Battle of Britain. During World War Two, Lord Nuffield's Cowley factories were the headquarters of 50 Maintenance Unit, which repaired hundreds of damaged aircraft.

Lord Nuffield (left), Princess Marina, the Duchess of Kent, and Mr S.V.Smith on a visit to the Cowley Car works on 3 July 1951.

Lord Nuffield tries his hand at archery at the Wingfield-Morris Hospital fête in the grounds at Headington in August 1952. What is now the Nuffield Orthopaedic Centre benefited hugely from Lord Nuffield's benefactions and he always took a keen interest in its work.

The millionth Morris Minor rolls off the production line in January 1961. It was the greatest British-made selling car in any class.

Left to right: the Warden of Nuffield College, D.N.Chester, Lord Nuffield, the Mayor of Oxford, Alderman H.G.L.Gordon Roberts
and the Duke of Edinburgh, when the Duke presented Nuffield College with its Charter on 6 June 1965.

Judith Lane outside her house at 16 James Street in March 1971, when the City Council erected a plaque to record Lord Nuffield lived there from 1896 to 1903.

FRANK COOPER'S OXFORD MARMALADE

In 1874 Sarah Jane Cooper made 76lb of marmalade on her kitchen range from an old family recipe. Her husband sold it at his grocery shop in High Street. It was so successful that in 1900 he opened a factory to make Cooper's Oxford Marmalade at the corner of Park End Street and Hollybush Row. The celebrated Oxford photographer, Henry Taunt, took these pictures there soon afterwards. This one shows the facade of Victoria Buildings.

Henry Taunt's shot of Cooper's preparation room.

The Packing Room at Cooper's Oxford Marmalade factory.

INDUSTRIAL ACTION

A rare picture of Oxford during the national General Strike from 3-13 May, 1926, when other trade unions came out in support of the miners, who were striking for higher pay. The railway workers had the biggest impact on Oxford, bringing both GWR and LMS stations to a virtual standstill – no joke in the days when a lot of goods, including milk and other perishables, travelled by rail as well as commuters. Motor vehicles – many driven by volunteer drivers – filled the gap and St Giles, as this picture shows, became a transport depot. It was also the setting for a lot of strike meetings.

Workers leaving Morris Motors Radiator factory in Bainton Road after deciding to join the strike in July 1956.

Cowley factory employees who continue to work run the gauntlet of jeering strikers in July 1956.

Les Davies, chairman of the joint shop stewards committee at the Cowley plant, taking a vote of confidence at a mass meeting outside
Morris Motors on 3 December 1958. Then men had walked out because of a rate fixing dispute.

Women members of the National Union of Vehicle Builders walk out of Morris Motors Cowley factory on 22 July 1959 after their union answers the strike call.

Morris Motors car workers attending a strike meeting at Cowley in August 1959 following the sacking of chief shop steward, Frank Horsman. The dispute, which lasted from 14 July to 12 August, was eventually settled by moving Mr Horsman to the Pressed Steel Company at Cowley.

Strikers at Morris Radiators attend an open-air meeting in May 1963.

Cowley car workers, made idle by the strike of Pressed Steel toolmakers, queue at Oxford Employment Exchange to draw unemployment benefit in April 1965. The strike for higher wages led to 5,200 car body workers being laid off at Cowley, 6,000 at Rootes in Coventry and smaller numbers at other plants.

Morris Motors workers attending a mass meeting on 20 September 1966 at the company's sports ground in Crescent Road.

Pressed Steel Company workers from Swindon picket the gates of the Cowley works in May 1967. They were among 1,300 dismissed by the firm at Swindon for striking unofficially for higher pay. They wanted the same rates as workers at Cowley.

Workers at Pressed Steel Fisher's Cowley factory queuing to sign on at the Labour Exchange in St Aldate's in April 1968. A Ministry of Labour spokesman said members of unions not on strike affected by the stoppage would get unemployment benefit. Strikers would not.

Car workers' wives protest at the activities of militant shop stewards at the Cowley plant in April 1974, behind the protective arms of a works policeman.

ON THE ROAD

The Abingdon-Faringdon coach about to leave the Randolph Hotel, Beaumont Street, at the turn of the century. The hotel, which opened in 1866, had its own stables.

A coach and four outside Magdalen College in 1912 about to take a party to a college point-to-point. The driver is Bill Organ of the Bear Lane Stables. At his side is Lord Ednam. Immediately behind him is the novelist, P.G.Wodehouse. On his right is Violet Hobson, mother of actress Valerie Hobson. Behind the driver is Oxford silversmith Richard Rowell.

Ancient and Modern Oxford. The out-of-date at the Cowley Road terminus represented by the horse tram, the up-to-date by the motor bus. The failure of the city to modernise its transport system prompted William Morris, later to achieve world renown as the car magnate Lord Nuffield, to introduce a private bus service with Frank Gray in November 1913.

The Reliance coach on its run between Woodstock and Oxford sometime before World War One. The steam traction engine is delivering a boiler from Edwin Danks and Co, Oldbury, Birmingham.

Workmen digging up the old horse tram lines in Walton Street in 1916. The metal rails were probably recycled. World War One was at its height.

W.H.Crapper's charabancs outside the Victoria Arms, St Bernard's Road, preparing to set off on a pub outing in the 1920s.

A Morris one-ton van in Gloucester Green in 1924 on its way to Elliston and Cavell's department store – now Debenhams – in Magdalen Street. The building is the old Central Boys School, later the bus company booking office.

The staff of Shotover House on their way to the 1924 British Empire Exhibition at Wembley in an old-fashioned, solid-tyred charabanc.

R.Brooks and Son, dairymen, of the Cinnaminta Road Dairy, Headington, delivering milk in 1930.

Wheelwrights at work in the 1930s. They heated the iron tyre in the furnace to make it expand, then banged it home over the wooden cartwheel. As it cooled, with the help of a few buckets of water, it contracted to produce a rigid structure.

The end of World War Two meant at last Oxford stores could replace their clapped-out delivery vans. A new Morris van outside All Souls College in May 1947.

A coach and four about to set off from the Clarendon Hotel, Cornmarket Street, early in the twentieth century. It was one of Oxford's best coaching hotels. During World War Two it served as an American servicemen's club. It was demolished in 1954.

BUSES AND TRAINS

Flooding under Station Bridge regularly blocked Oxford's main road to the west until the introduction of water pumps.
This was the scene at the Great Western Railway Station in 1875 when the water under the bridge must have been as deep as the
River Thames beyond.

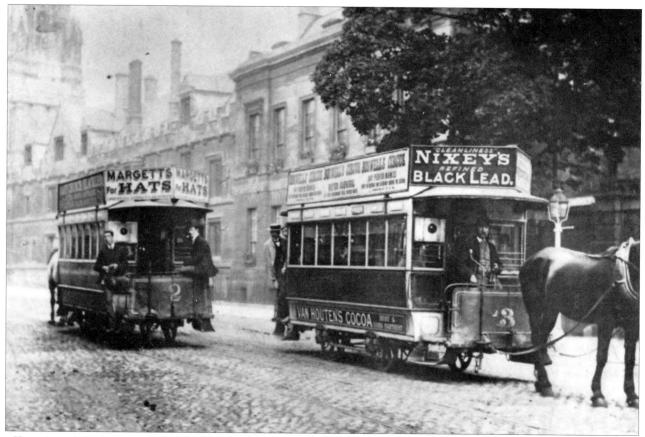

Horse trams in High Street, Oxford, in the early 1900s. Plans for their replacement by electric trams foundered because the colleges
objected to unsightly overhead cables at the heart of the university city.

A city horse bus, which reached the places Oxford Tramway Company's horse trams could not, at the Iffley terminus early this century. The driver was Alfred Gardner.

The interior of what was then still the London and North Western Railway Station in 1914. Built by the same team responsible for Crystal Palace in 1851, it employed a similar cast-iron and glazed structure. It became the LMS Station in 1922 when the LNWR was taken over by the London, Midland and Scottish Railway.

Single and double-decker buses at the Cowley Road terminus about 1914. The future Lord Nuffield forced the city to modernise its antique public transport system by introducing private motor buses to compete with the horse trams and buses in 1913.

The Oxford-Charlbury bus with driver and conductor in the early 1920s when such vehicles still had solid tyres.

City of Oxford Motor Services employees at the Cowley Road garage in March 1928.

The London, Midland & Scottish Railway Station at the corner of Park End Street and Rewley Road. It closed to passengers in 1951.

A typical Saturday lunchtime
bus queue in Cornmarket Street,
Oxford, at 12.40pm on 25
January 1955.

South Midland Motor Services reintroduced topless
buses to Oxford in August 1957 to enable tourists
to see the sights.

Five young train spotters at Oxford Station in 1958.

Oxford Railway Station platform looking south in June 1968.

Buses queuing to take
Pressed Steel workers home
in November 1959.

Gloucester Green Coach Station in July
1962. Behind the café is the bus station. In
the foreground is the car-park.

Waiting at Oxford Railway Station on 23 December 1964.

Morris Motors workers arriving at the Cowley works by bus for the day shift in June 1966.

The last of a dying breed: bus conductors Madge Grant, June Allen, Jim O'Donoghue and Mary Doherty in December 1974. Once every City of Oxford Motor Services bus had a driver and a conductor, who issued your ticket. By the time this picture was taken there were only 22 'clippies' to 35 drivers. Soon there would be none.

The Gloucester Green bus and coach station café in September 1975 – a picture prompted by an *Oxford Mail* reader's protest about its shabbiness.

TENDING THE SICK

The entrance to Cowley Road Hospital in July 1968. It looked after about 200 elderly patients.

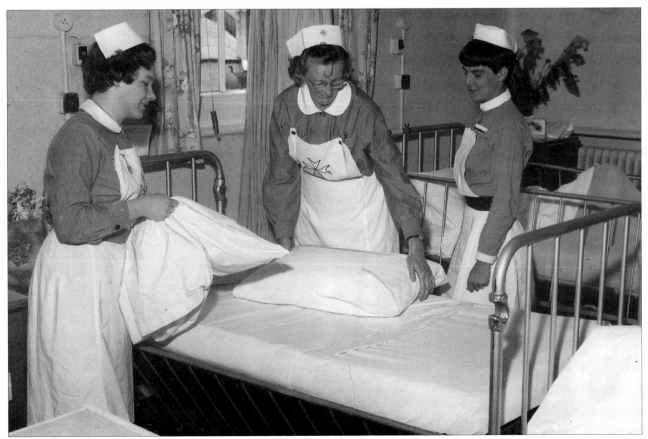

Auxiliary nurses Jane Porter (left) and Anne Storpmenn making beds under the supervision of sister Jane Danson at Cowley Road Hospital in August 1967. It cared for the elderly.

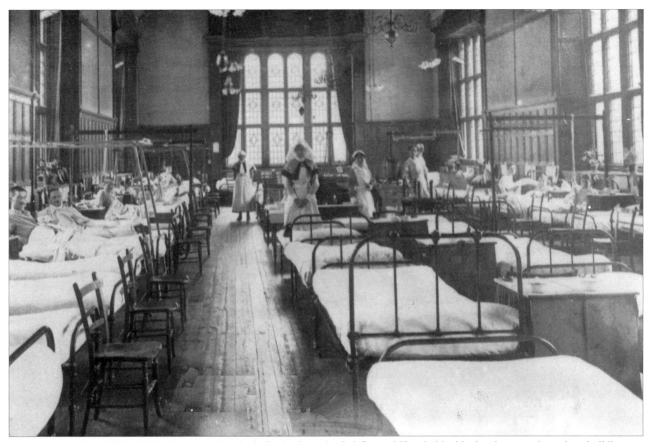

Many casualties of World War One ended up in Oxford, where the 3rd General Hospital had its headquarters in various buildings around the city. This picture shows a surgical ward at the Examination Schools.

The plaster room at Cowley Road Hospital.

Logic Lane – a place for a therapeutic stroll. It led to the nurses' quarters.

Across High Street from the Examination Schools, the Masonic Buildings later The Forum dance hall – were also pressed into service to provide hospital wards.

Convalescing servicemen
sunning themselves in the
grounds of Cowley Road
Hospital.

A tented ward in New College Gardens. Fresh air was considered a great healer.

The boot shop at Cowley Road Hospital, formerly the city workhouse. The convalescents were probably not repairing military footwear but learning a trade which might prove useful in peacetime.

OXFORD'S ESTATES

Barton, north-west of the Oxford Ring Road at Headington, has been a settlement since Saxon times but, following World War Two, it mushroomed into one of Oxford's largest housing estates. This is Bernwood Road in 1956.

Some of the steel, asbestos-lined 'prefabs' on the Barton estate in July 1958.

At a Green Belt inquiry in September 1961, the council houses on Barton estate were described as 'unfortunate' and
'remarkably ugly'.

Green Road roundabout, Headington, with Barton beyond in November 1969.

Some of the prefabs came down in 1971 – to the disgust of the proprietors of the Underhill Circus shops beyond, who complained of loss of trade.

Barton in the snow in January 1977.

Although the Barton estate had plenty of critics, Oxford City Council did better with the Blackbird Leyes housing estate, started in the late 1950s east of the Oxford Ring Road between Rose Hill and Cowley. This picture shows a terrace of three-bedroomed homes in August 1960.

A group of shops at Blackbird Leys in August 1960.

Windrush Tower, the first of two 15-storey blocks of flats at Blackbird Leys, under construction in September 1961.

Windrush Tower nearing completion on 21 February 1962. It was opened by Geoffrey Rippon, of the Ministry of Housing and Local Government, on 9 April. In the background Evenlode Tower is well under way.

Percy Lewis, former British
Empire featherweight boxing
champion, invests 16-year-old
Ann Bradford with her sash as
the Belle of Blackbird Leys in
July 1964.

Michael and Patrick Moloney about to pass Michael Hall and Trevor Reason in the soap box Derby at Blackbird Leys Festival in
August 1966.

OXFORD CHURCHES

Cornmarket Street and St Michael at the North Gate Church in 1885. Zacharias's, on the right, was famous for its mackintoshes.

The City Church of St Michael at the North Gate in flames on 9 October 1953. The fire was started in the organ by an arsonist. The church was unusable for nearly a year.

A visitor surveys the gutted interior in December 1953. But outside an illuminated Christmas tree greeted shoppers as usual.

Repair work under way in March 1954.

If you want to know the time ask a fireman. Oxford Fire Brigade restoring the hands to the newly illuminated clock face of St Michael at the North Gate Church tower. The Saxon tower, built about 1050, is the oldest building in Oxford.

The interior of S.S.Phillip and James Church as it looked at the end of the nineteenth century. Popularly known as Phil and Jim, it was built in the 1850s to meet the spiritual needs of expanding North Oxford.

The exterior of S.S.Philip and James Church in April 1962.

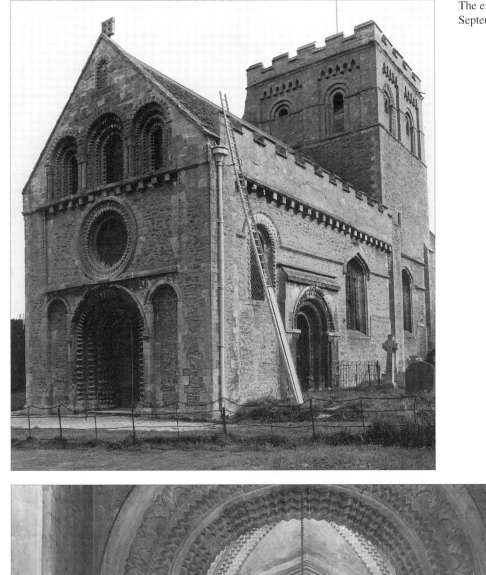

The exterior of Iffley Church in September 1960.

Iffley Church in October 1960 when concealed floodlighting was introduced to show off the exquisite Norman arches and vaulted roof.

The altar of St Aloysius Roman Catholic Church, 25 Woodstock Road in January 1932. At the service of dedication in November 1875, Cardinal Manning, in a famous sermon, berated the University for abandoning

A workman removes statues during restoration work to the reredos behind the high altar in the chancel of Christ Church Cathedral in July 1960.

The Bishop of Buckingham, the Right Revd G.D.Savage, with youngsters at the Children's Whitsuntide Gifts service in Christ Church Cathedral in June 1963.

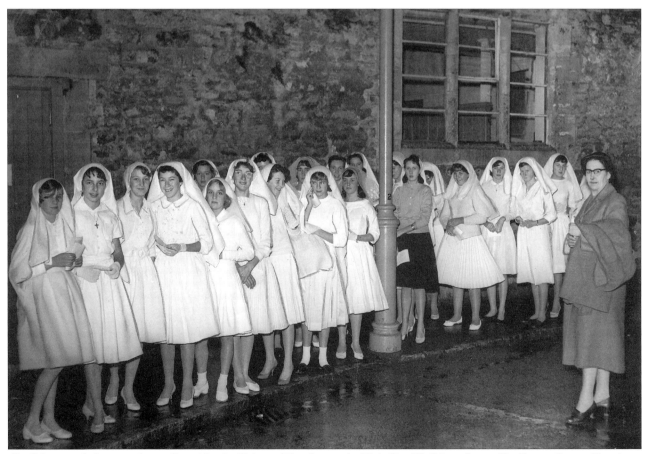

Candidates on their way to be confirmed by the Bishop of Dorchester, the Right Revd D.G.Loveday, at Headington Quarry Church on 8 December 1959.

Hospital workers at the Oxford Regional Hospital Board service of dedication and thanksgiving in the University Church on 20 September 1959.

SOME ROYAL CONNECTIONS

Visit of the Queen to Oxford on 11 March 1921. Front row (left to right): Princess Mary, Vice-Chancellor L.R.Farnell, Queen Mary, the Chancellor Lord Curzon, Mrs A.L.Smith and Mrs A.H.Johnson. Behind: Miss Moberly of St Hilda's, the Warden of All Souls' College F.W.Pember, Lady Ampthill, the President of Magdalen College Sir Herbert Warren, the Master of Balliol College A.L.Smith, the Dean of Christ Church Dr H.J.White, Countess Curzon, Miss Jourdain and Sir Harry Verney. The chalk marks on the wall refer to Balliol College rowing eight's success in the spring Torpids.

Queen Mary on her way to the Sheldonian Theatre to receive an honorary degree on 25 June 1932.

The future Queen, Princess Elizabeth, visiting Oriel College with the Provost, Dr G.N.Clark, while in Oxford on 25 May 1948 to receive the honorary degree of Doctor of Civil Law.

Princess Margaret in fur stole leaving Blenheim Palace with the Duchess of Marlborough (in black hat) to attend a garden party in Blenheim Park in June 1953, the month of her sister's Coronation. Sir Winston Churchill (extreme right) was born in Blenheim Palace and was a frequent visitor.

Crowds waiting outside the entrance of the new library at Lady Margaret Hall on 4 November 1960 for the Queen to open the new building. During her visit she also laid the foundation stone of the new St Catherine's College.

Prince Charles and Princess Anne leaving Shotover House for a tour of the Country Landowners' Association Game Fair in Shotover Park on 30 July 1965.

Princess Marina at the bedside of five-year-old Andrew Wallace of Aylesbury during her visit to the Nuffield Orthopaedic Hospital, Oxford, in April 1961.

The Queen chatting to
students in the Junior
Common Room at Oriel
College, where she presided
at dinner as Visitor of the
college on 2 May 1968.

The Prince of Wales representing
Cambridge at the Inter-Varsity Polo
Match at Kirtlington Park on 9 June
1968. The Queen presented the Cup to
Oxford, who won 2-1.

The Queen meets Councillor Olive Gibbs in St Ebbe's on 2 May 1968 when she inspected the plans for the new Westgate development. Mrs Gibbs told the Queen that women councillors brought logic to the City Council 'which the men haven't got'.

IMPORTANT VISITORS

Winston Churchill, the man who was to become Britain's World War Two leader, in bow-tie, and other newly-initiated members of the Albion Lodge of the Ancient Order of Druids under the branches of one of the oldest oaks in Blenheim Park. The ceremony took place in August 1908.

Winston Churchill in camp as a young man with the Oxfordshire Yeomanry about 1910. Standing left to right: Major Viscount and Winston (W.S.) Churchill. Sitting: the Duke of Marlborough and Winston's brother, John Churchill.

Sir Winston Churchill receives the freedom of Woodstock from the Mayor of the Borough, the Duchess of Marlborough, in August 1947.

Sir Winston Churchill chats to Lord Charles Spencer-Churchill, younger son of the Duke and Duchess of Marlborough, before leaving Blenheim Palace after a visit in July 1959. Also in the picture are Mr Edward Russell, husband of Lady Sarah Churchill, and the Duchess.

Crowds queue to see Sir Winston Churchill's grave in Bladon Churchyard after his death in January 1965.

Senator Robert Kennedy is mobbed by cheering crowds in Cornmarket Street on 28 January 1967. The US Attorney-General and brother of assassinated President John F.Kennedy came to Oxford to address students in the Union Debating Hall while attending an Anglo-American conference on European Unity at Ditchley Park. Eighteen months later, he, too, was shot dead.

Earl Mountbatten on his last visit to Oxford in 1975 to unveil a plaque at the Dragon School, where his twin grandsons, Timothy and Nicholas Knatchbull, were pupils. Timothy was killed with his grandfather and Nicholas critically injured in an explosion in 1979.

Field Marshal Lord Alexander of Tunis, Lady Alexander and the President of Trinity College, Mr A.L.P.Norrington, after the Field Marshal had unveiled a new statue of the college's founder, Sir Thomas Pope, in September 1955.

Not content with cutting the cake to mark the 30th anniversary of the Oxford charity's Oxfam's Shop in Broad Street in November 1977, Margaret Thatcher doles out a slice to Oxfam director Brian Walker. The Conservative Party leader and future Prime Minister was in Oxford to visit the Cowley motor plant. Beside her is the Oxford MP John Patten, who was destined to follow in her footsteps as Secretary of State for Education.

The Indian premier Jawaharlal Nehru at Oxford Station in February 1961 with Philip Whitehead, president of the Oxford Union, before speaking at the student debating society,

Another Indian premier, Mrs Indira Gandhi, who was an undergraduate at Somerville College, waves to the crowds outside the Clarendon Building in November 1971. She was in Oxford to receive an honorary degree.

John Masefield, the Poet
Laureate, who lived at
Boars Hill, at Milham Ford
School in May 1955 with
the headmistress, Miss
M.R.Price, and (extreme
left) Miss Rose Bruford.

Sir John Betjeman, later Poet Laureate,
opening the Dragon School fête in June
1964.

A chameleon helps top naturalist Peter Scott welcome the nature film company, Oxford Scientific Films, to their new studios at Long Hanborough in November 1970.

Solo flyer Sheila Scott at Oxford Airport with chief engineer Les Baston checking out her twin-engined Piper Aztec for a round-the-world trip in April 1971.

The Beatles in Oxford. The world famous pop group came to Oxford on 5 March 1964 as part of a campaign by student Jeffrey Archer, now better known as the best-selling author, to raise £1m for the charity, Oxfam. They dined at Brasenose College, to which Mr Archer was attached, with the Principal, Sir Noel Hall. Here pictured in the exclusive student club, Vincent's, are (from left to right) Ringo Starr, George Harrison, Paul McCartney and John Lennon. Jeffrey Archer is half visible to the left of Paul.

Police try to hold back Beatles fans.

Above, left: Richard Burton and Elizabeth Taylor with Professor Neville Coghill in February 1966. They had just arrived to begin rehearsals for Professor Coghill's production of Marlowe's Dr Faustus at the Oxford Playhouse. Richard Burton played Faust. Liz Taylor was Helen of Troy. Right: Arriving for the premiere of the film version of Dr Faustus in October 1967. It took place at the ABC Cinema, now the MGM George Street.

Prizewinner Pippa Lay of Brightwell-cum-Sotwell receives her award from Dame Margot Fonteyn at Blackwell's Bookshop in February 1980. The legendary ballerina was in Oxford to sign copies of her book, *The Magic of Dance*.

Above, left: The conductor, Sir
Thomas Beecham, arriving to deliver
the Romanes Lecture at the
Sheldonian Theatre with the Vice-
Chancellor A.H.Smith in June 1956.
Right: Actress and former ballet star
Moira Shearer tries her hand at
bowls at Oxford Liberal Party fête in
July 1959.

Elizabeth Sweeting, manager of the Oxford
Playhouse, greets actress Vivien Leigh when
she attended a matinée performance of
A Passage to India in February 1960.

The director and star of the film version of Harold Pinter's *The Caretaker* at a lunch at the Mitre Hotel to mark the Oxford showing in June 1964. Left to right: Bill Maelor-Jones of the Moulin Rouge Cinema, Headington, director Clive Donner, actor Donald Pleasence, and Eric Bowtell, managing director of the Scala Cinema, now The Phoenix Picture House, Walton Street.

Comedian Spike Milligan cuddles up to an inflated Mrs Thatcher during a show at the Apollo Theatre in September 1982.

Taking a lunchtime break in George Street: actors Edward Woodward, Dame Judi Dench and Leo McKern. The trio were rehearsing for the English premiere of Ferenc Molnar's *The Wolf*, which opened at the Oxford Playhouse in August 1973 and went on to become a West End hit.

Actor James Robertson Justice at the Oxford Union with Eric Abrahams, president of the university debating society, and another guest speaker in October 1964.

The prospective Parliamentary candidate for North Paddington – alias comedian Jimmy Edwards – after addressing members of Oxford University Conservative Association in January 1964. He was playing Merry King Cole in panto at the New Theatre and took time out to do a little light-hearted politicking at the Newman Rooms.

Film star Zsa Zsa Gabor arrives – late as usual
– for lunch at Blenheim Palace in June 1964.
With her is her then husband, Herbert Hutner.

Top of the Pops presenter Allen
(Fluff) Freeman at the opening of
a new shop in Cowley Centre in
January 1963.

The veteran Headington Quarry Morris dancer, William Kimber, then 87, cuts the tape in October 1958 to open the crescent named after him at Headington. It was a chance meeting between the stonemason and Cecil Sharp in 1899 which led Sharp to record old English folk songs and dances and save them from oblivion.

Olympic athlete Mary Rand takes a fancy to the press photographer's motor cycle at Iffley Road Running Ground in February 1964.

OXFORD CHARACTERS

Oxford's oldest college servant, Dick Cadman, or 'Cadders' as he was known to generations of students, retired after nearly 67 years service on 8 February 1968 – his 94th birthday. Here 'Cadders' is pictured in June 1962 with three of the gentlemen he looked after. Arthur Bown (right) and his two sons, James (left) and Mark, had returned to Oxford to receive their MA degrees.

You never left 'Cheddar' Wilson without an apt quotation from Shakespeare. The Oxford engine-driver seemed able to recite the entire works at will. He played football first for St Frideswide's Boys, later for Cowley, and later still was an ardent supporter of Pegasus, who, to his eternal delight, won the FA Amateur Cup. But above all he loved swimming. He celebrated his 65th birthday by swimming from Folly Bridge to Iffley. Here he is taking his daily dip at snowbound Long Bridges in January 1960.

Oxford's 'reliable top hat man' Jimmy Dingle, who died in 1970 at the age of 84, started life as a barrow boy but after World War One became a billboard man and tireless fund-raiser for charity. He is pictured here between the wars at St Giles's Fair, raising money for the Radcliffe Infirmary.

A weir keeper in the traditional clothes of his calling at a weir on the Thames above Oxford early this century. Henry Taunt, who photographed him, wrote: "What old Harper didn't know about the weeds, the fish and the wild ducks, wasn't worth knowing."

Three Oxford characters of earlier years. Left to right: 'Dobber', who earned a precarious living busking to theatre queues. Among songs he sang were *Pretty Polly Perkins of Paddington Green* and *To Be A Farmer's Boy*; Cabman Jimmy Meade, who had a stand at the cab rank opposite Magdalen College. Among his regulars was the Prince of Wales, later King Edward VIII, when he was a student there shortly before World War One; Cyprian – 'Syfe' – Harris, who earned his living as a gofer at the covered market running errands for tradesmen and holding the reins of horses. The money he left paid for a splendid funeral and a memorial in Botley Cemetery.

Radio Oxford presenter Bill Heine with the shark that has adorned his roof in New High Street, Headington, and defied the best efforts of the planners to remove it, since 1986.

THE CUTTESLOWE WALL

Oxford's answer to the Berlin Wall – the Cutteslowe Wall. The Urban Housing Company erected the two 7ft-high walls surmounted by revolving spikes in December 1934 to prevent residents of Oxford City Council's Cutteslowe estate in North Oxford from walking through its own private housing development. It meant Council tenants had to make a detour of nearly a mile to reach the Banbury Road.

A communist firebrand, Abe Lazarus, led the first attempt to demolish the walls in May 1935, arguing that the walls were in breach of the City by-laws. But the Chief Constable warned that anybody attempting to demolish the walls would be arrested for assaulting his officers and the attempt failed.

The campaign continued in Parliament and the courts. In 1938 a Parliamentary Committee led by Sir Stafford Cripps, ordered the company to destroy the walls. It refused so the Council moved in and demolished the walls on 7 June 1938. The company then took out a High Court injunction. In 1939 the courts decided in its favour and up the walls went again.

During World War Two a tank demolished one wall and a car damaged the other. But, despite protests that the walls made life difficult for air-raid wardens, both were rebuilt. It was not until Oxford City Council bought the two nine-inch strips of land on which the walls were built, for £1,000, that the way was clear for their demolition. On 2 March 1959 Councillor Edmund Gibbs, watched by his wife, Olive Gibbs, ceremonially swung the pickaxe.

And children from Cutteslowe Primary School made history as the first people to officially walk through the gap.

THE EMPEROR HEADS

A section of the wall and railings round the Sheldonian Theatre is replaced by a wooden gate in September 1958 to let the builders in.
Thanks to the Oxford Historic Buildings Appeal Christopher Wren's architectural gem was completely restored between 1959 and 1964.

The Oxford sculptor, Michael Black, at work on new Emperors' Heads for the Sheldonian Theatre in September 1972. He maintained they represented various styles of beard.

OXFORD'S MARKETS

From the eighteenth century until 1932 Gloucester Green was the place to sell your cattle in Oxford. It was still a very important market when this picture was taken in 1895.

Until the second half of the eighteenth century the greengrocers, butchers, fishmongers and the rest who supplied the university and city sold their wares at markets in the central streets of Oxford. The Covered Market which opened between High Street and Market Street in 1774 was designed to bring them all under one roof. The Chancellor of the University had control of the market until 1889 and Clerks of the Market continued to operate until World War One. Here Dr C.H.O.Daniel, Provost of Worcester College, checks the weight of a pound of butter at Ernest Pigott's shop in 1909.

Ernest Pigott's shop in the Covered Market as it appeared in a booklet to mark the millenary of Oxford in 1912.

Alderman Lady Townsend, Mayor of Oxford, switching on the Christmas decorations at the Covered Market in December 1958.

Weighing cheese at the Covered Market in December 1958. It is celebrated for the quality of its provisions.

The Covered Market in 1959.

Hedges the Butchers displaying their Christmas fare in the Covered Market in December 1983. The side of beef on the left of the picture came from the first prize-winner at a major fatstock show.

Because cattle and sheep were clogging up the city centre the Oxford Cattle Market moved to the Oxpens in 1932. It gradually dwindled in importance and by the time this picture was taken sometime after World War Two had become a distinctly modest affair.

At the beginning of the 1980s the Oxpens Market closed to make way for the expansion of the Oxford College of Further Education and the market traders returned to Gloucester Green. Shoppers looking for bargains at the last market in the Oxpens on 28 July 1982.

Back at Gloucester Green: the market in full swing in August 1982.

FAIRS IN OXFORD

A Bible stall outside St John's College at St Giles's Fair in the 1880s.

St Giles's Fair, a general view looking north in 1906. People flocked to the fair from all over Oxfordshire and youngsters in service came home from places further afield.

Gloucester Green Fair. General view of the south side showing the Corn Exchange Hotel, roundabout and stalls in May 1908.

Street fairs were commonplace before the arrival of the motor vehicle. St Clement's Fair in 1910 looking west towards the Plain. The swings and roundabouts were further east.

St Clement's Fair. Looking away from the Plain showing stalls and the crowd in the road, about 1910.

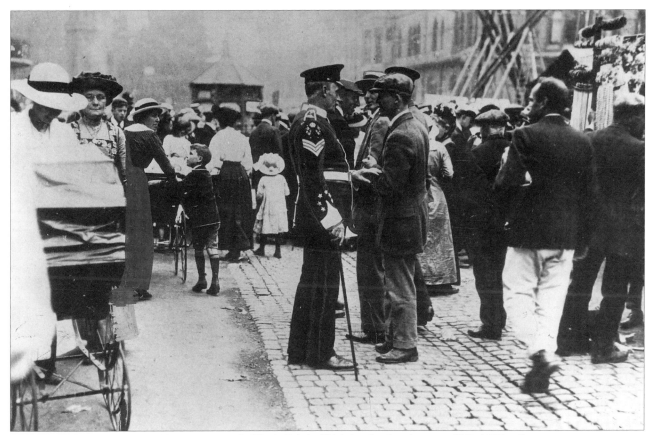

The recruiting sergeant at St Giles's Fair in 1914 shortly after the start of World War One.

Mrs Bird's gallopers at St Giles's Fair in the 1920s when cloche hats were all the rage and the fare of two old pennies was an awful lot of pocket money.

The Wild West Show at St Giles's Fair between the wars.

The 'clockwork man' – what we should now call a human robot – attracting the crowds at St Giles's Fair on 4 September 1957.
Oxford's biggest and last surviving street fair still closes St Giles to traffic for two days every September.

CUSTOMS & FIESTAS

Osney ox roast in 1887, probably to mark Queen Victoria's Golden Jubilee.

Headington Quarry sheep roast in 1899.

Beating the bounds is a traditional way of recording parish and city boundaries and teaching them to the next generation, hence the frequent use of choir boys to carry out the operation. This photograph shows beating the bounds of St Peter in the East parish in Merton Street, 1908. The church in Queen's Lane is now part of St Edmund Hall.

A party of civic dignitaries crossing the Seacourt Stream by the North Hinsey Ferry whilst beating the boundaries of Oxford City at the turn of the century.

The Rector of what was then still the City Church,
Canon R.R.Martin, sets off from All Saints under
an archway of canes to beat the parish bounds in
May 1955. Notice the predominance of women in
the party. The church is now Lincoln College
Library.

A party of choir boys from St
Michael at the North Gate Church
beating the bounds at Frewin Hall
on Ascension Day, 1975. The man
in the mortar board is the rector of
the church, the Revd Norwyn
Macdonald Ramm.

Sheep roasting at Headington Quarry in November 1961 to commemorate the dedication of Holy Trinity Church on 22 November 1849. The annual ceremony was dropped in 1914 because of World War One, but revived in 1959 by local enthusiasts.

The Sheriff of Oxford, councillor J.B.Tompson (centre) before setting off on his annual drive of Port Meadow, in July 1954. Freemen of Oxford and Wolvercote commoners have the right to graze their beasts on the city's largest expanse of common land, which was mentioned in the *Domesday Book*. Once a year the sheriff and his posse round up the animals. Owners with rights can retrieve them for a nominal fee. Those without are fined, lending to a municipal office a brief Wild West romance.

The last animal to be rounded up in the 1963 drive, a yearling called Pixie. Notice the mounted officer of the Royal Society for the Prevention of Cruelty to Animals on the left and the police car bringing up the rear.

The 1971 round-up. The ceremony takes place unannounced, usually in the early morning. Hence the mist on Port Meadow this April morning.

MAY MORNING

Nowhere is the ancient fertility rite of May Morning celebrated more vigorously than in Oxford. At dawn choristers climb to the top of Magdalen College tower to sing their 6am invocation to summer as their predecessors have done for centuries. And the streets below are filled with Morris dancers and merrymakers determined to make the most of the annual festivity. Hardly any of them give a thought any more to whether the crops grow. It remains an occasion when the past spills over into the present. This picture shows nineteenth-century mummers with Jack-in-the-Green outside Balliol College in 1886.

Schoolchildren celebrating May Day at Iffley about 1910.

The May King and Queen process through the streets of Iffley in 1959.

Students on the River Cherwell at Magdalen Bridge listen to the May Morning hymn from the top of Magdalen College Tower in 1962.

A university Morris man astride his hobby-horse leads the procession up High Street after the May Morning hymn.

May Day rallies are also a tradition of the Labour Party, although usually at a more civilised hour than the medieval rite of spring. Holding the City Labour Party banner as the procession crosses Magdalen Bridge in 1963 are Albert Fagg and Olive Gibbs. To the right of Councillor Gibbs is Evan Luard, Labour MP for Oxford. Behind him is Gerry Fowler, a city councillor also destined to become an MP.

Serenaded by bagpipes, battered gramophones and wistful jazz revellers who have been up all night awaiting the May Morning hymn.

Inevitably a lot of revellers fall in. And sometimes, as in 1966, an entire punt load capsizes.

East Oxford Junior School dance The Blaydon Races during the school's May Queen celebrations in 1967.

Morris men performing for the May Day crowds outside the New Bodleian Library in 1970.

The Iffley May procession in 1967.

Children from Donnington Junior School performing a maypole dance in the grounds of Iffley Church as part of the village's May celebrations.

Crowds on May Morning run into several thousands if the weather is fine. Here are some of them at the bottom of Broad Street in 1976. People perched anywhere they could to get a better view of the Morris dancers performing on the forecourt of the New Bodleian Library.

OXFORD'S THEATRES AND CINEMAS

The façade of the New Theatre in George Street in 1886. It had been a theatre site since 1836, when the Victoria Theatre, later the Theatre Royal, opened its doors.

The New Theatre, now the Apollo Theatre, in George Street. The present theatre, built in 1933, is Oxford's largest with a capacity of 1,800. This picture was taken in February 1964.

The former big game museum in Woodstock Road, which was the home of the Oxford Playhouse from its inception in October 1923 until it moved to its present theatre in Beaumont Street in October 1938.

The Beaumont Street façade of the Oxford Playhouse.

The Playhouse foyer at Beaumont Street in April 1956.

The former New Picture Palace in Jeune Street. It opened in 1911, closed in 1918, but had a second lease of life as the Penultimate Picture Palace from 1976 to 1994.

The Oxford Electric Theatre in Castle Street, looking east towards Queen Street. Frank Stuart, the proprietor of the East Oxford Theatre in Cowley Road, opened Oxford's first cinema on 26 November 1910. It was quickly followed by five others. It closed in 1923.

The Electra Palace cinema in Queen Street in 1913. A notice in the foyer states members of the university are 'admitted to one shilling seats only' – in other words the most expensive.

The Oxford in Magdalen Street. It advertised itself as the super Oxford Cinema when it opened in 1924 and the Super Cinema quickly became its name. It is now the MGM Magdalen Street, Oxford's largest cinema.

Super Cinema manager Denis Cave makes his feelings clear about vandalism at the Magdalen Street picture house in October 1960.

The Electra Palace in Queen Street in 1934 when the main attraction was *The Lodger*. It opened in 1911.

Ten local dalmatians and their owners turn up for the first showing of Walt Disney's *One Hundred And One Dalmatians* at the Ritz, George Street, in August 1961.

The entrance to the East Oxford Theatre in Cowley Road, a popular variety venue at the turn of the century. Its proprietor, Frank Stuart, had been showing film shorts between the music-hall acts since 1900. In 1912 he rechristened it the Palace Theatre and it survived as a cinema until 1938. This picture was taken in January 1954.

The scene inside the ABC Cinema, George Street, Oxford, after fire gutted the interior on 11 March 1963. It opened in 1936 as the Ritz and is now the MGM George Street, divided up into three studios.

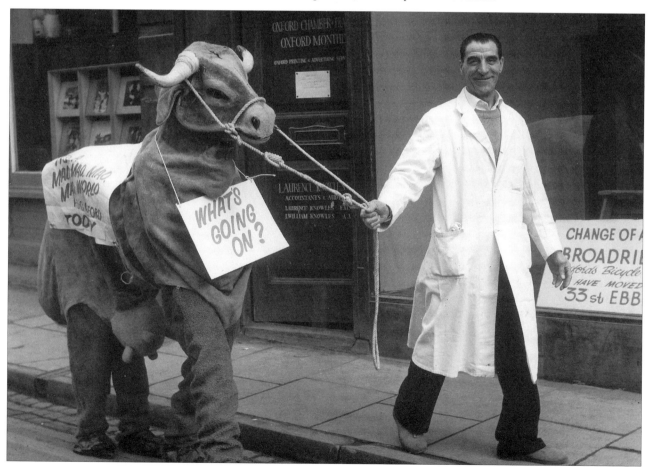

Advertising the film *It's A Mad, Mad, Mad, Mad World* at the ABC Oxford in March 1965.

ABC Cinema manager Jack Frost makes a farewell presentation to 20-year-old John Sharp in October 1965 to mark his promotion to second projectionist at the Regal Cinema, Cowley Road. The Regal is now a bingo hall.

Ronnie Hilton, starring in *Goody Two Shoes* at the New Theatre (now the Apollo Theatre), Oxford, signs autographs for children attending the first ABC Minors matinée at the ABC Cinema in January 1972.

Workmen converting the ABC Cinema in George Street into three studios in October 1975. ABC One opened in November, ABC Two and Three followed in December.

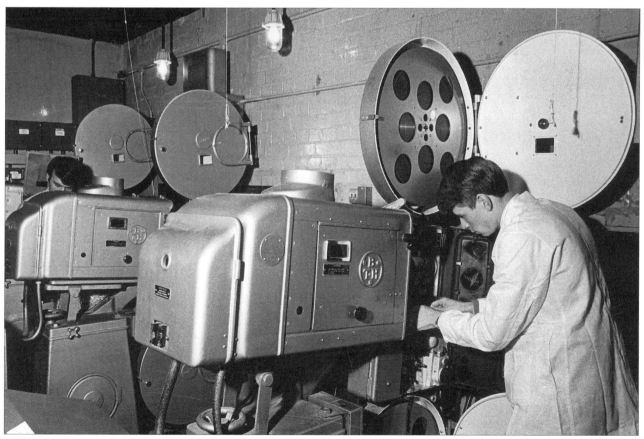

Chief projectionist Roy Cox prepares for the opening of Studio 1 and Studio 2 in Walton Street on 28 December 1970. Oxford's oldest surviving cinema started life as the North Oxford Cinema in 1913. It became the Scala Cinema in 1920, Studio One and Two in 1970, the Phoenix Cinema in 1977 and the Phoenix Picture House in 1994.

'The Phoenix cinemas [seen here in 1970] in Walton Street have failed in a bid to show films to the public until 2am each morning. The application was turned down by the City Council's Environmental Health and Control Committee at a special meeting, but it will make no difference to the cinema's opening hours. Phoenix One and Two will remain open until 2am for public performances three nights a week, and for performances for club members only on the other four nights, as at present. A unanimous vote by the committee went against the Phoenix after a petition was handed in signed by about 40 residents in the Walton Street area complaining about the behaviour of students attending the late-night films.'
Oxford Mail, 27 November 1980.

The New Cinema, Headington, which opened in 1923. It was later known simply as Headington Cinema. In 1960, when it changed hands, it became the Moulin Rouge and in 1980 the Not the Moulin Rouge. This picture was taken in 1961 when it was showing *Carry On Constable*.

DANCING IN OXFORD

The Forum as it looked in 1967. At one time it was the mecca of ballroom and modern dancers in Oxford – a recognised place for boy to meet girl.

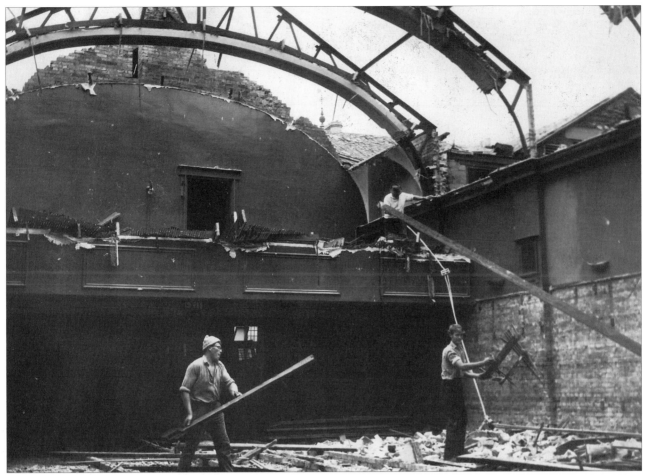

Workmen demolishing the Forum Dance Hall in High Street in July 1965. The last dance took place there on 19 June that year. The hall made way for a £500,000 extension to St Edmund Hall.

One of the 18 beat groups taking part in a beat talent show at the Carfax Assembly Rooms in June 1964.

A contestant makes the most of his three-minute break during a six-hour rock 'n' roll dance marathon in St James Hall, Cowley, in April 1960. Two of the 30 couples kept going to the end.

Mohamad Nasseri and Valerie Holland on their way to becoming the Best Twisters In Oxford at the Town Hall in January 1962.

Doing the Gay Gordons at the Oxford Council of Drama and Music ball at the Randolph Hotel in October 1959.

Members of the English Folk Dance and Song Society performing on the lawns of St John's College in July 1964. Some 400 members attended the Society's annual dance.

OXFORD BANDS

The Oxford Accordion band in March 1938.

Morris Motors Band at the Albert Hall in October 1938 when they came fourth in the championship section of the *Daily Herald* Brass Band Championships.

The Pressed Steel Band leading several hundred boy scouts from St Giles to St Aldate's Church for a St George's Day service in April 1958.

OXFORD'S PARKS

A workman puts the finishing touches to a shelter with a mosaic tiled floor in Headington Hill Park in April 1959. It was formerly the dairy of Headington Hill Hall. The City bought the estate in 1953 and later rented Headington Hill Hall, now part of Oxford Brookes University, to Robert Maxwell. The park they laid out as a woodland garden with over 150 ornamental trees and specimen shrubs.

Cutting the grass in Headington Hill Park in May 1957.

Sowing grass in South Park, the opposite side of Headington Road to Headington Hill Park, in September 1955.

Children enjoying the swings and
roundabout at Bury Knowle Park in
August 1962.

Ten-year-old Elizabeth Cattle and Amanda
Warmington from Wood Farm quenching their
thirst at the drinking fountain in Bury Knowle
Park in October 1963.

Tulip display in Florence Park in May 1955.

Gardener L.Allsworth watering the bowling greens at Florence Park in June 1957.

Children enjoying the paddling pool at Florence Park in August 1962.

TAKING A DIP

Charles Cox, the proprietor of the Parson's Pleasure bathing place, aged 88, pictured on 26 May 1913. Swimming costumes were not necessary at the all-male establishment.

Tumbling Bay bathing place pictured around 1955.

New Hinksey School PE instructor Mrs S.D.Meeson, teaching pupils the backstroke at Hinksey Pool in May 1959. Because of maintenance and staffing costs the pools no longer open until the summer school holidays.

A bather taking the plunge at Hinksey Pools with a little help from her friends during the August Bank Holiday in 1961.

The now defunct Long Bridges bathing place beside the Thames between Folly Bridge and Iffley in August 1965.

SPORTING OXFORD

Skipper Ron Atkinson and manager Arthur Turner (right) in mutual congratulation at the news that Oxford United have drawn Preston North End during the club's great FA Cup run of 1964, when they became the first Fourth Division side to reach the quarter-finals.

Oxford firemen pumping water on to the parched Manor Ground pitch in August 1964.

Volunteers helping to clear United's snowbound ground in January 1967.

An aerial view of Oxford United Football Club's Manor Ground in Headington in February 1967.

Manager Arthur Turner hugs skipper Ron Atkinson after United clinch promotion to Division Two in 1968.

Oxford City Fire Brigade covering the Manor Ground in foam in an effort to protect it from frost in January 1970.

Police move in after a wall collapses during Oxford United's FA Cup clash with Watford in January 1971.

Groundsman Les Bateman covers the Manor Ground with straw in January 1972 to protect the pitch from frost before United's FA Cup-tie against mighty Liverpool.

Led by skipper Dave Roberts, the United team emerge from the tunnel for a practice session. The tunnel was part of a £45,000 development under the stand including the building of new dressing-rooms in the autumn of 1974.

Millionaire Oxford publisher Robert Maxwell became a hero when he stepped in and rescued Oxford United from bankruptcy in January 1982. But the new chairman tarnished his image a year later when he suggested the club should merge with Reading to form a club called Thames Valley Royals. While he was in charge United climbed from the Third Division to the First and in 1986 won its first major knockout trophy, the Milk Cup. A fan asks for the new chairman's autograph.

Robert Maxwell attempting to quell a riot at the Manor in September 1982 during a tense top-of-the-table clash with Portsmouth. A record 61 people were arrested and seven policemen were injured.

Fans make their feelings clear about Robert Maxwell's plan to merge United with Reading in April 1983.

Fans sharing a moment of triumph with Robert Maxwell in December 1983.

A team of 40 volunteers clear the Manor pitch of snow in February 1985 in a vain effort to enable United's match with Shrewsbury to go ahead.

Malcolm Shotton, the Oxford United captain, receives the Milk Cup after United's 1986 Wembley triumph.

Applying 345 tons of sand to the United pitch in 1987 to improve drainage.

Throughout the 1950s the toast of Oxford soccer was Pegasus FC, a team of Oxford and Cambridge students, formed by Sir Harold Thompson in 1948. Among other exploits they reached the quarter-finals of the FA Amateur Cup no less than five times and won the trophy twice, packing Wembley Stadium for the Finals. In 1951 they beat the famous North-East club, Bishop Auckland, 2-1 at Wembley, and in 1953 crushed Harwich & Parkeston 6-0 in the Final. In this picture, Pegasus centre-forward J.S.Laybourne is foiled by the Harwich goalkeeper B.King.

In Februay 1949, Oxford fans of Pegasus queued for hours in Turl Street to purchase tickets for the FA Amateur Cup fourth-round tie against Bromley at Iffley Road.

Roger Bannister breasts the tape at Iffley Road, Oxford, on 6 May 1954, to record the world's first sub-four minute mile.